PRAISE FOR *A STEADY RAIN*

"Huff elevates to tragic dimensions the life of policemen the way Arthur Miller moulded Willy Loman in *Death of a Salesman* . . . *A Steady Rain* is the most potent new play on Broadway." —BAZ BAMIGBOYE, *Daily Mail*

"*A Steady Rain* offers one of the most powerful theatrical experiences in many seasons . . . Huff's script is full of pungent dialogue and razor-sharp suspense." —DAVID SHEWARD, *Back Stage*

"[Huff] has taken very familiar subject matter—the morally ambiguous life of cops working the mean streets—and made it seem fresh, authentic, brutally uncompromising yet not sensationalized . . . The taut, 90-minute script builds with a tragic inevitability, yet with a coda of redemption that seems neither forced nor fake." —RICHARD ZOGLIN, *Time*

"Extraordinarily visceral . . . [An] exceptionally rich, gritty and emotional drama . . . [*A Steady Rain*] will get you right where you live." —CHRIS JONES, *Chicago Tribune*

"Briskly absorbing . . . Denny and Joey are drawn with such earthly wit and non-patronizing compassion that *Rain* never rings false or superficial." —ELYSA GARDNER, *USA Today*

"The power of A *Steady Rain* lies in its honesty and pathos . . . At once powerful and explosive . . . A *Steady Rain* marks the broadway debut of an important new voice."
—FERN SIEGEL, *The Huffington Post*

"Engaging, gritty and even poetic . . . Thoroughly intense . . . Not to be missed." —MATT WINDMAN, onoffbroadway.com

"This is theatre as stripped-down story-telling; a two-hander played out on a sparse set over a gripping 90 minutes . . . By turns humorous, dark and tense."
—CLAIRE STENHOUSE, *The Daily Telegraph*

"We've seen characters like the men in A *Steady Rain* before— frustrated city patrolmen dreaming about making detective, maybe bending the law a little yet convinced they're doing an honest job. And we've seen variations on their downward spiral and partner conflict in gritty cop shows . . . But playwright Keith Huff recharges those familiar elements by approaching events usually outlined in action terms with the probing eye of a forensics investigator and psych profiler combined."
—DAVID ROONEY, *Variety*

"Combine the profound, terrifying sorrow that defines the bloodiest of Greek tragedies and the contemporary urgency of the latest Chicago police brutality scandal and you've got some idea of the emotionally eviscerating potency of Keith Huff's A *Steady Rain*. Told in 90 minutes by two characters on a stage that's bare but for a table and two chairs, the stark power of

Huff's drama is all-consuming, a syringe of Mexican Mud with a China White chaser shot straight to the heart."
— CATEY SULLIVAN, *Windy City Times*

"[A] tightly intertwined story of two men who are like brothers. Huff tells the story of a relationship of almost biblical intensity, and one riddled with love, loyalty, guilt, shame, rage and a sort of primal inevitability . . . Superbly rendered, often deeply poetic." — HEDY WEISS, *Chicago Sun-Times*

"There are no heroes, nothing more superhuman than big-fisted talent in *A Steady Rain*, Keith Huff's dark, moody, small but brutal 90-minute duet . . . A tight, mean story about a petty, mean world . . . The writing is . . . commanding, with a bully-boy swagger and a closely observed sense of casual ugliness." — LINDA WINER, *Newsday*

"[*A Steady Rain*] is a thoroughly engrossing examination of the toll the job takes on those sworn to serve and protect, and how amorphous the line between criminal and cop can be." — BARBARA VITELLO, *Daily Herald*

"With one eye zeroing in on neo-noir crime drama and the other targeting the emotional complexities of male friendships . . . Keith Huff's *A Steady Rain* hits its dramatic targets with point-blank precision." — BRIAN KIRST, *Chicago Free Press*

GEORGETTE HUFF

KEITH HUFF

A STEADY RAIN

Keith Huff is a resident playwright at Chicago Dramatists, earned an MFA from the Iowa Playwrights Workshop, and is the recipient of a Jeff Award, the Cunningham Prize for Playwriting, the John Gassner Memorial Playwriting Award, the Berrilla Kerr Award, and three Illinois Arts Council Playwriting Fellowships. His plays have been produced off Broadway, internationally, and nationally. Recent productions include the critically acclaimed smash hit *The Bird and Mr. Banks* at the Road Theater in Los Angeles, *Pursued by Happiness* as part of the First Look Festival of New Plays at Steppenwolf Theater, *Gray City* at American Repertory Theater, *Dog Stories* at Stageworks/Hudson, *Harry's Way* and *Prosperity* at Riverside Theater, and *Karaoke Night at the Hog* at Chicago Dramatists. He lives in Chicago with his wife, Georgette, and his daughter, Robin.

A STEADY RAIN

A

STEADY

RAIN

KEITH HUFF

FARRAR, STRAUS AND GIROUX

NEW YORK

FABER AND FABER, INC.
An affiliate of Farrar, Straus and Giroux New York
120 Broadway, New York 10271

First edition, 2010

Library of Congress Cataloging-in-Publication Data
Huff, Keith, [date]
    A steady rain / Keith Huff.—1st American ed.
        p. cm.
    "Originally produced by New York Stage & Film/Powerhouse, 2006."
    ISBN 978-0-86547-936-4 (pbk. : alk. paper)
    1. Police—Illinois—Chicago—Drama.   2. Friendship—Drama.
    3. Crime—Illinois—Chicago—Drama.   4. Chicago (ill.)—Drama.   I. Title.

PS3608.U34968S74 2010
812'.6—dc22

                                                         2009041762

Designed by Abby Kagan

www.fsgbooks.com

P 1

ACKNOWLEDGMENTS

As with any collaborative undertaking, many, many people generously lent time and talent to the development of A *Steady Rain*. To them my heartfelt thanks:

Fred Zollo, Barbara Broccoli, and Michael G. Wilson.

Robert Cole.

Michael Rose and Jeffrey Sine.

Daniel Craig and Hugh Jackman.

John Crowley.

Randy Steinmeyer, Peter DeFaria, Russ Tutterow, Brian Loevner, Troy West, and everyone at Chicago Dramatists.

Josh Stamberg, Adam Rothenberg, Trip Cullman, Liz Timperman, Leslie Urdang, Max Mayer, Mark Linn-Baker, Beth Fargis Lancaster, Johanna Pfaelzer, and everyone at New York Stage and Film.

Larry Mitchell, Brant Spencer, K. Lorrel Manning, Lee Brock, Seth Barrish, and everyone at the Barrow Group Theater.

John Buzzetti, Barry Kotler, Frank Wuliger, Eric Garfinkel, and John Bauman.

Bob Freedman and Marta Praeger.

Richard Hoover.

Harold C. Hieber.

John Buzzetti again . . . because some people deserve to be thanked twice.

Most of all, Gigi and Robin for their love and support.

A STEADY RAIN

PRODUCTION HISTORY

A *Steady Rain* was originally developed in a series of table readings and staged readings at Chicago Dramatists (Russ Tutterow, Artistic Director; Brian Loevner, Managing Director).

The play was first presented by New York Stage and Film (Mark Linn-Baker, Max Mayer, Johanna Pfaelzer, Leslie Urdang, Producing Directors; Elizabeth Timperman, Executive Director) and the Powerhouse Theater Program (Beth Fargis Lancaster, Executive Producer) at Vassar, July 2006. The production was directed by Trip Cullman.

DENNY	Josh Stamberg
JOEY	Adam Rothenberg
STAGE MANAGER	Julie C. Miller
SCENIC DESIGN	Richard Hoover
LIGHTING DESIGN	Matthew Richards
COSTUME DESIGN	Katherine Roth
SOUND DESIGN	Jill BC DuBoff
PRODUCTION MANAGER	Peter L. Smith
CONSULTING PRODUCER	Bob Boyett
CASTING DIRECTOR	James Calleri, CSA

A *Steady Rain* received a workshop production at the Barrow Group Theater (Seth Barrish and Lee Brock, Co–Artistic Directors), February 2007. The production was directed by K. Lorrel Manning.

DENNY	Brant Spencer
JOEY	Larry Mitchell
STAGE MANAGER	Dawn Hillen
PRODUCTION COORDINATOR	Isaac Klein
PRODUCTION DESIGN	Travis McHale
COSTUME DESIGN	Jim Hammer
ASSISTANT DIRECTOR	Josh Mendelow

A *Steady Rain* had its professional world premiere at Chicago Dramatists in fall 2007. The production was directed by Russ Tutterow.

DENNY	Randy Steinmeyer
JOEY	Peter DeFaria
STAGE MANAGER	Tom Hagglund
SCENIC DESIGN	Tom Burch
LIGHTING DESIGN	Jeff Pines
COSTUME DESIGN	Kerith Wolf
SOUND DESIGN	Mike Tutaj

The Chicago Dramatists' production was remounted at the Royal George Theater in 2008 and received Joseph Jefferson Awards for Best New Work, Best Production, and Best Actor (Randy Steinmeyer).

A *Steady Rain* opened on Broadway at the Schoenfeld Theater (produced by Frederick Zollo, Michael G. Wilson, Barbara Broccoli, Raymond L. Gaspard, Frank Gero, Cheryl Wiesenfeld, Jeffrey Sine, Michael Rose Ltd, The Shubert Organization, Inc., and Robert Cole) on September 29, 2009. The production was directed by John Crowley.

DENNY	Hugh Jackman
JOEY	Daniel Craig
PRODUCTION STAGE MANAGER	Michael Passaro
SCENIC AND COSTUME DESIGN	Scott Pask
LIGHTING DESIGN	Hugh Vanstone
ORIGINAL MUSIC AND SOUND DESIGN	Mark Bennett
STAGE MANAGER	Pat Sosnow
COMPANY MANAGER	Lisa M. Poyer
PRODUCTION ASSISTANT	Alison M. Roberts

CHARACTERS

Joey, a Chicago cop
Denny, his partner

THE TIME AND PLACE

The not-too-distant past. Chicago.

THE SET

Minimalism is called for . . . the suggestion of an inter-
view room.

NOTES

A *Steady Rain* is a duologue. Joey and Denny speak directly to
the audience and tell their story, which, from time to time, is not
exactly the same story. At times they are testifying before an in-
ternal affairs review board. At times they are vying with each
other for credibility. Both characters have Chicago accents.
They also habitually drop words and occasionally make words
up and speak in redundancies (sometimes a typo is not a typo).
Please, trust the script as written. Joey and Denny also occasionally address each other, in which instance a formal scene oc-
curs. Parenthetical shifts in address are not always indicated in
the text. It should be obvious from the context whether Joey and
Denny are addressing the audience or each other. The light
changes noted throughout also indicate movement changes.

1

Lights rise on DENNY *and* JOEY.

DENNY We just signed on as a Nielsen family, yunno, the
ratings guys? They come into your home and attach this,
the fuck, this box to your TV. And when you watch, all you
do you pass around this remote and whoever's watching
what, they punch in they're watching, right? They hooked
a box up to the TV in Noel's room. There's even one
buttoned up to the black-and-white kitchen set and the
38-inch boober me and Connie got in the boudoir. So the
first night we got it, Connie and the kids and me, we're
lounging around in the family room figuring out how we
can push all these buttons at once. Yunno, really screw up
the Nielsen guys? And my partner, Joey, he's over, I explain
to him what's the deal. And he tells me . . .

JOEY You go pushing more than one button at a time, Den,
you're not screwing anybody. You're just canceling
yourself out.

DENNY The fuck do you know, you fuckin' mick? Are you
screwing anybody presently?

JOEY Same thing you vote Democrat and Republican the
same election. And besides . . .

DENNY . . . Einstein continues . . .

JOEY Them Nielsen guys pay more attention to toilets
flushing during commercials than to any frigging box.

DENNY And I tell Joey he's fulla shit. Which he is usually.
'Cause, I mean, is he a Nielsen family? The elbow-bender
still lives in this one-room chinch pad looking over an
alley. Never married, not even dating, for Chrissake, so
his chances of even having a family let alone being lucky
enough to get the call from Mr. Nielsen and enlisted into
the privileged ranks are pretty slim, yunno what I mean?
So, of course, he puts down the value of being a Nielsen
family 'cause people, friend or foe, they do this all the
time consistently. They put down what you got 'cause they
don't got it 'cause they wish they had it but they don't.
Even shits like Joey. I known the guy since kinnygarten.
He puts down marriage, kids, big-screen TVs, everything
that has value that he don't got 'cause if it has value that
makes him a very poor man by comparison.

JOEY So Denny's on his way to the fridge for another Bud
Light, laying into me for dumping on his conspicuously
acquisitive lifestyle again, when all a sudden the front
pane window explodes in like this huge spiderweb of
splinters.

DENNY Hole big as a nut at the center.

JOEY And across the family room the screen on the
big set . . .

DENNY . . . the 52-incher, the one we just knobbed on hock
from Best Buy to make a good impression on the Nielsen
people . . .

JOEY . . . it explodes, too.

DENNY Nobody knows what the hell is up, glass falling all
over my wife and kids, Joey diving over them to cover
them best he can.

JOEY Heinz was barking at the TV set 'cause it's still, you know, sputtering fireworks and smoke.

DENNY I had to yank out the plug and collar Heinzy and by this time Connie is screaming 'cause there's all this blood.

(The lights change.)

JOEY Things were already pretty choked that night before the bullet hit. Denny'd made up his mind to reform me. We'd both been passed over the third time in a row on detective promotions, I'd been half-fractured most the time since and Denny refused to let me put my life on the rocks about cowplop of that particular ilk.

DENNY Best friends since kinnygarten. It's only right.

JOEY Now, I don't know the Department has a quota system.

DENNY Fuck they do.

JOEY Denny says they do.

DENNY Believe me, they do.

JOEY I don't know. I do know I aced that detective exam the third time in a row . . .

DENNY We both did.

JOEY . . . and fifty guys with lower scores got upped to plainclothes ahead of me.

DENNY Fifty guys upped to the ranks of dickhood with not only lower scores and less service but who just all happen to be a lot more ethnic than me and my bog-hopping amigo paisan over here.

JOEY I'm not saying there's reverse racism.

DENNY Fuck if there ain't.

JOEY But Captain Dickerson . . .

DENNY The supreme dick of all dicks.

JOEY . . . he's had it out for me and Denny ever since we went through the Department grievance procedure and forced him to remove reprimands he'd tucked in both our files. The reprimands were for racist remarks and sure, Denny and me, knocking around in the locker room might have let slip a rude word or two about the apparent injustice of this unstated quota system.

DENNY But Dickerson's cheese-eating rat patrol overhearing something not even intended for their fuckin' ears gives the man no right to put reprimands in our files that can effectively stonewall our careers.

JOEY So I was blitzed a lot . . .

DENNY A lot? Joey, you were spoon-feeding yourself sterno for breakfast.

JOEY . . . and Denny, to keep me off the sauce, he talked Connie into having me over just about every night of the week.

DENNY We kind of adopted the mutt. Heinz took a shine to him.

JOEY I appreciated the gesture. It was a good thing to do. Denny was always doing things like that, always looking out for people. He was a good guy. A people person.

DENNY You show a nonstarter like this the good life, beautiful house, beautiful wife, beautiful kids, a dog, all these TVs, it can have kind of a reformative effect, right?

JOEY Did me anyway. Only Denny, he'd bring these women to dinner night after night trying to fix me up. He brought this one woman Rhonda over. A hooker. I know this for a fact because I'd seen Denny taking money from her out

on patrol. Nothing inherently bad in that. A dozen or so
hookers, he looked after them and they greased him. In
exchange, he wouldn't run them in, keep the pimps off
their backs.

DENNY Hey, I enabled those girls to keep just about most
what they made, exactly the way free enterprise in this
country should be.

JOEY Like I said, Denny was a stand-up guy. But this
Rhonda . . . what a trip. Denny, he thought the kind of girl
I'd fall hard for was Rhonda's type. When actually she's
more the type he'd go for. Which was one of his faults, I
guess. It was apparent from the first moment we all sat down
at dinner what was up. Connie was bringing in food, tossing
Denny the fisheye. And Denny's getting all pissed off at me
because I don't talk to Rhonda. And Rhonda, I don't know,
she's sensitive, I guess. Three glasses of wine, she's stuffing
her face, she never ate food like it, complimenting Connie,
spitting chunks of half-chewed lasagna across the table
onto Stewy's high-chair tray. Then she starts in about her
childhood, which, believe me, was no Disney movie. When
Rhonda brought up incest at the dinner table, that was it
with Connie. She left the room. Denny's shouting after her:
"Get back to the table, be civil, we got company!"

DENNY That's me . . . ?

JOEY That's you.

DENNY You're doing me.

JOEY I'm doing you. But Connie was a good match for
Denny because she wouldn't take any of his shit. I always
thought that about them. They were a good couple. So
Connie gone, who does Denny lay into next?

DENNY I told Joey, I told him: it's perfectly logical. To start a new life, person's got to make new friends, right? Rhonda don't get exposed much to the good life. I want to expose her to the good things, give her a taste of how good the good things can be. It's you all over again, Joey. You got no right to look down. Everybody at this table knows you got a fairly severe drinking problem.

JOEY Den.

DENNY Okay, well, hey, so maybe Rhonda didn't know till now. But she's company. And besides, I bring you to our table night after night for the same logical purpose. You get exposed to the good life suddenly, the bottle in your case, making a living flat on your back in Rhonda's, it don't look so fuckin' appealing, right? Am I right? What? What I say?

JOEY Fortunately, the phone rang. So Denny, before he answers it, he tells us:

DENNY Sure, the fuckin' phone rings, drop everything just to yap with some fuckin' scammer wants to sell me *TV Guide*. You two entertain yourselves, okay?

JOEY And he leaves me and Rhonda there alone at the dining-room table. I couldn't think of anything to say. Neither could Rhonda, I guess. But while we were sitting there, out the corner of my eye, she's sitting next to me, I could see her bottom lip start to quiver like she's going to cry. But before she did, she runs out the front door with her coat. Denny comes back into the dining room jumping for joy because he got called to be a Nielsen family, but then the smile drops from his face and he asks me:

DENNY The fuck is Rhonda?

JOEY She split.

DENNY And how you suppose she's supposed to get home, uh?

JOEY Didn't she drive?

DENNY No, she did not drive. The general idea, shit-for-brains, is you give her a lift home. One thing, another, land the green, sink the putt, a family guy, uh?

JOEY You promised you weren't gonna do this anymore, Den.

DENNY The fuck is wrong with you, Joey? She's a nice girl.

JOEY Did I say she wasn't?

DENNY Did you say she was? All night, you're Buster Fuckin' Keaton with the silent bit. Dipshit didn't say two words to her all night. I told him, it don't just happen, Joey. You got to make a fuckin' effort. Great woman like Connie don't just fall into your lap. And you know what the lowlife tells me?

JOEY I told him, Rhonda is not Connie, Den.

DENNY As if I don't know the fuckin' difference. What, he thinks I plucked Connie newborn in her birthday suit out the Virgin Spring when I married her? She had a history same as Joey, same as me, same as Rhonda. I told him that.

JOEY And I said, it's not the same thing and you know it.

DENNY What are you, a lawyer? Correcting me, what I say, what I think, you know what this is?

JOEY I got to go.

DENNY A double fuckin' standard!

JOEY Oh, is that what it is?

DENNY It's a double fuckin' standard, J. Rhonda's had a hard life.

JOEY We're all doing hard time at the Rock, Denny.

DENNY Harder than any lumps you know.

JOEY Save it for the pulpit, okay?

DENNY That girl lays her life on the line just to make it day-to-day out on the streets and you dish her off beyond redemption?

JOEY All right, don't shut up.

DENNY You tell me it's not them and us? Rhonda ain't one of us, uh?

JOEY Denny grabbed his coat and told me:

DENNY Tell Con I'm taking Rhonda home.

JOEY . . . and stormed out the door.

(The lights change.)

JOEY This bit about them and us? Sergeant Wallace, he suggested maybe to get on Dickerson's good side before the next detective promos are made, me and Denny, we maybe take this race-relations seminar the Department is offering free, no charge. So I sign up, but Denny, he's too busy being a family man and all, and he asked me to coach him on what they teach me, you know, watch his back so he don't let anything remotely mean-spirited slip in the locker room like before. So I do, I did. And we're busting these two gangbangers, these Latino and African-American gentlemen. We caught them pants down with all this pharmaceutical grade H and coke—morphine, too, a fishing-tackle box fulla vials. We load the haul into the squad-car trunk, the cuffed gentlemen into the backseat, and up front I tell Denny, the names he called these guys while we were reciting them their Mirandas, he should be a little more cautious. That's all I said. And he gets all defensive.

DENNY Say what, what I say?

JOEY The words, Denny, the words.

DENNY What, I said it to you, Joe. Polite company, you're my goombah, my partner in crime. What, are you gonna tell on me?

JOEY The trick is to not even think those words, Den.

DENNY Think 'em? What, you want inside my fuckin' brain, now, you Irish tampon?

JOEY You asked me to help you on this, I'm helping you.

DENNY How can I not think what I'm thinking, Joey?

JOEY I'm only saying, Den.

DENNY It's all I heard our neighborhood since day one.

JOEY Forget about it, okay?

DENNY You, too, Joey. You know the neighborhood. My ma, my dad, they barely had fifteen words of fuckin' English between 'em, these included.

JOEY Don't get a hard-on about it.

DENNY Who's getting a hard-on?

JOEY You're getting a hard-on about it.

DENNY How can I not fuckin' think what I'm fuckin' thinking?

JOEY It offends people, okay?

DENNY And I'm not offended you tell me something's wrong the way I think. Something evil inside me?

JOEY Nobody said evil, Den. Who said evil? Who?

(*Pause.*)

DENNY Nobody, okay? But I'm maybe as sensitive as this gangbanging ethno-shit in the backseat, maybe I take it that way.

JOEY Den.

DENNY They get more sensitive, I should be less?

JOEY Den.

DENNY They want tolerance from me they should start tolerating my *in*tolerance.

JOEY It's not them and us, okay? That's what I mean, okay?

DENNY You don't know what the fuck you mean.

JOEY We're all the same, Den, all right?

DENNY You are the egghead. I am the walrus.

JOEY Don't denigrate it, now.

DENNY Personally, I don't cogitate transcendental shit like that so well (*punching* JOEY), so I punched the fuck.

JOEY Ow.

DENNY And I told him, keep your koo-koo-ka-chew shit, Joey. You know what PC fly ball said to me?

JOEY You've got to quit hitting people, too, Denny.

DENNY What, you're all sensitized, too, now? I love you, Joey. What do you want me to do? Hug and kiss you in public?

JOEY Knock it off, Den.

DENNY Wub you wittle tumtum?

JOEY You don't realize how hard you hit.

DENNY (*Punching* JOEY.) What, that?

JOEY Knock it off!

DENNY Oh, he's so sensitive. (*Wraps* JOEY *in a headlock and gives him a knuckle sandwich.*) So sensitive you could use him to wipe a wittle baby's bottom.

JOEY (*Pulling away.*) Will you effing knock it off, Denny!?

DENNY *Effing?* Excuse me, *effing?* Would that be with one Fs or two, Officer Friendly? Please at least pay me the respect of swearing like a man in front of me or not at all. (*Pause.*) What a baby.

JOEY It's not about being a baby. It's about you treating people better.

DENNY Oh, you take a seminar in Racial Speak and suddenly you're Mr. Fuckin' Rogers?

JOEY Maybe so, yeah, sure, why not?

DENNY You might think it, but that seminar ain't gonna make one flyshit fleck of difference your detective app comes up again 'cause you're the wrong fuckin' color, spud.

JOEY I'm making an effort, okay?

DENNY Shits bust my balls day and night with this pasta basta wop shit.

JOEY It takes an effort, Denny.

DENNY Do I file a lawsuit? Issue a fuckin' reprimand? You and me, we take it on the chops 'cause it's funny, we got a sense of humor about it, it's the way things are. So, please, I don't wanna subject it to any more of your narrow-minded, neo-Nazi bullshit this afternoon 'cause I'm trying to do my job and drive a fuckin' squad car over here, all right?!

JOEY Then drive!

DENNY I'll drive when I'm fuckin' ready to drive! (*Pause.*) So, hey, Poindexter, you still coming over to dinner tonight or is your spoon arm too wounded? (*Pause.*) Connie's making lasagna. (*Pause.*) Douche bag. (*Pause.*) C'mon, Joey, hey.

JOEY I got things to do, Den.

DENNY Things, what things? Rearrange the affordable portables around that one-room roach motel you call home?

JOEY I been over too much lately.

DENNY My kids love you, Connie loves you, I love you, Heinzy loves you. Your right leg, anyway. We want you there.

JOEY It's your family, Den. I'm all the time in the way.

DENNY Joey, we grew up together. We're partners. You're family. I care about you. I don't want you going back to that armpit of a bachelor pad and sticking it to a bottle of Schnapps tonight.

JOEY Can't you ever give it an effing rest?!

DENNY My ears, please, I'm sensitive. Hey, you got a problem with the bottle, I got a problem with my mouth. We're helping each other out, right? Right? We're gonna be detectives together someday, Starsky and Hutch, this is good for us, right? I look out for you, you look out for me. Back to back, Joey. Come on.

JOEY No way I'm coming over if you're trying to fix me up again.

DENNY You asked me never again. Would I do that to you?

JOEY That was the night he fixed me up with Rhonda.

(The lights change.)

JOEY After Denny stormed out to drive her home, I went
upstairs to give Connie his message. She was in Stewy's
nursery looking out the window. She looked so beautiful
holding him, you know, the way moms do. Room was
dark. Moonlight on her face. Stewy conked out on her
shoulder. I tiptoed over, brushed Stewy with the back of
my finger on the cheek and saw out the window what
Connie saw. Denny was out in the driveway with Rhonda.
She was crying full out by then. Denny was, you know,
consoling her. Connie didn't like that one bit. It started to
rain that night, I remember. I don't think it let up more
than a minute or two till this whole mess was over.

(Fade.)

2

Lights rise on DENNY.

DENNY This thing with Rhonda, Jesus, driving her home
   after dinner, she's snotting up the dashboard of my
   Plymouth the whole way 'cause she's embarrassed in
   fronta Connie and Joey, the kids and me 'cause she spit
   food across the table and something about her breasts,
   some mammary malfunction, both spigots leaking
   through her blouse or some shit. I told her I'm married,
   Ronnie, I got kids, I seen leaky tits before, it's nothing to
   get in Dutch about. Hey, if there's one thing Rhonda
   should not be ashamed about, it's her upper frontal
   superstructure. Make that two things. Man. She slapped
   me with a wet one on the cheek to thank me for cheering
   her up and waggled her heart-shaped pillow of a derriere
   into this shit-heap tenement where she lived.
      When I went in after her, I kept thinking the place
   should be fuckin' condemned. I followed Rhonda up to
   her door and when I knocked, it swung open. Shit side of
   Uptown and not even a working lock on the door. Rhonda
   had slipped outta her blouse and was bending over a
   dresser drawer. Out of it she lifted up this tiny baby and
   started breast-feeding it. She had this tiny baby and she'd
   left it all this time closed up in a sock drawer so she could
   come over to my place and socialize. She might have seen

me coming 'cause when she turned toward me, no top on, the baby glommed on to gazunga number two, she didn't look too surprised. Christ, it was a beautiful sight. Like some fuckin' stain-glass Madonna. Rhonda told me close the door. I did. I just watched her with the baby. After a minute or two, she took me by the hand and led me to her bed. Out of our clothes in a second, she pulled me into her from behind and she kept breast-feeding her kid. Sounds fuckin' perverted, but believe me, it was the closest thing I had to a religious experience since my First Communion.

I handed her some cash as I was leaving but she took it the wrong way. I told her I didn't mean it that way. She's putting the kid back to sleep in the drawer and I told her the money was for her and the kid, I'd get her more, anything to keep her off the streets, 'cause I had no idea she had a kid to take care of, it broke my heart. It fuckin' did, I mean it. Rhonda wouldn't look me in the eye when I tossed the money by the dresser, but I meant what I said. I'm full of shit in many respects, but one-on-one I always keep my word.

So I'm back out in the Plymouth and a piece of brick the size of my fist shatters my windshield. I seen this kid no more than ten or eleven running, so I pull my service revolver and run after the little fuck in the pouring rain. He ducks down an alley, and me, my mind full of Rhonda and Connie, my windshield, my kids, it don't even hit me this yard rat's leading me somewheres till a broomstick swings out at me from behind a dumpster and thwacks me square across the chest. Dead in my tracks, winded, I fall

back, my service revolver goes flying, and this slimy pimp
piece of shit named Walter Lorenz jumps out from
behind the dumpster, the man behind the broomstick.
He calls to the kid: "The gun, Willy! Grab the gun!" and
comes at me twirling the stick like a baton, one end of
it sharpened and charred like a giant number-2 pencil.
Walter tells me: "Not much of an escort without your
piece, are you, Officer Lombardo?" I had dealings with
this fuck a hundred times before. Last time, Rhonda's
jaw cracked, her eye swollen shut, I recognized Walter's
handiwork and had it out with him, told him I'd shoot
him on sight next time I saw him. I shoulda seen this
coming, which is always nice to say in hindsight, right?
    Walter tells Willy keep the gun trained on me while
he comes jabbing at me with his black-tipped broomstick,
telling me it's been a long time since he had shish-kebab
cop in this part of town. He tells me I mess with Rhonda,
I'm messing with more than his property. I'm messing
with his income, which, in these parts, is a small matter
of life and death to some people. Walter jabs at me again
with the broomstick. Barely able to breathe, I roll away,
clutching my chest. Bruised three ribs, it felt like, one of
'em cracked. Then, just as I was stumbling to my feet,
reaching for Willy with the gun, Walter jabs at me again
and sticks me deep in the thigh. My whole head went
white and I must have let out some kinna scream 'cause
when I could hear again, Walter's jumping up and down
in the alley laughing his ass off how he got me squealing
like a stuck pig. Walter came at me again, this time at
my chest, but I backhanded the point of the stick away,

yanked it crosswise toward me and Walter along with it so
hard I clocked him one square in the jaw with the top of
my head. He got the worst of it. I got a pretty hard head.
Off balance, I tossed him to one side and slapped him
across the face a time or two with the stick. Three or four
times, maybe, I don't remember. I swung around on my
good leg and was actually about to drive the point end
of that stick through his fuckin' eyeball when he shouts
to Willy: "Shoot the motherfucker, Willy! Shoot!"

I didn't stick him but I shoulda. Hindsight, again.
Instead I snapped the broomstick in half and chucked the
pieces over a fence. Then I limped over to Willy, my hand
out, asking for my service revolver. He's got it locked on
me, both hands shaking, all the time Walter, his coach,
his mentor, prodding him on with: "Shoot him, Willy!
Shoot him, you pussy wimp shit motherfucker!" All the
time I clocked on the streets of Chicago, you can see it in
the eyes. I dunno what it is. Something dead in the eyes
tells you the person behind the trigger means business.
Willy didn't have it. Not yet. I just took the gun away from
him. I asked him: "This your friend?" By this time he's
crying. He's just a kid. His brother, he tells me. "Your
brother put you up to throwing that brick?" "Yessir," he
says. Walter chimes in: "Don't talk to him, Willy! Just shut
the fuck up!" Willy tells me Walter told him if he threw
the brick at my car he'd get him a puppy. So Walter
tells Willy: "No way you're ever getting a puppy now,
chickenshit!" Something died in Willy's eyes just then.
Sometimes that's all it takes. Then he ran off. With my
good leg, I kicked Walter across the jaw for that last crack.

It's a habit with me. I like to have the last word. Plus, this abusive crap breaks my heart, yunno?

When I got back that night, Joey's sleeping on my family-room couch, Connie's laying a blanket over him. I ask her doesn't this eight ball ever go home? Right off the bat she lays into me: "Where the hell you been, Denny?" I tell her I'm a cop, it's a twenty-four-hour job. Then she sees all the blood. She helps me to the bathroom, starts tugging at my pants. I tell her: "I can do it, Connie! Christ, lay off of me!" A little too forceful, maybe, yeah. 'Cause where I been, what I done, I can't stand her near me, touching me. She knows it, too, the way I can't look her in the eye. Backing out she tells me: "All right, Denny, do it yourself! You're the man of the family! Do everything yourself!" My pantleg was soaked with blood. In the middle of my right thigh was this deep black hole the size of a nut. I swung my right leg into the bathtub and grabbed the bottle of rubbing alcohol off the back of the toilet. I poured it on and my head went white all over again. But I didn't scream, I didn't shout. I bit hard into a towel and took it 'cause, I dunno, my sons were sleeping and they rely on me to be strong for them, yunno? And in a strange way, I was glad for the pain and wished it woulda hurt worse. I mean, I betrayed Connie that night and I felt deep down I deserved it.

(*Fade.*)

3

Lights rise on JOEY *and* DENNY.

JOEY The bullet through Denny's front window made perfect
sense with all the dirt he'd gotten into lately out on patrol.

DENNY I was on duty that night and me and Joey, we'd just,
yunno, stopped by to grab something to eat, make sure
the Nielsen boxes were working, and good thing we did.

JOEY The blood was from Stewart mostly. Stewy we call him.
He's Denny's youngest. He's about two.

DENNY When the shards of glass fell, I couldn't get to
Connie and the kids as fast as Joey did on accounta my
leg. And if Joey hadn't covered them the way he did, it
coulda been much worse, believe me.

JOEY Noel and Connie got cut up on their hands and arms
from reaching out to cover their heads from the falling
glass.

DENNY I grabbed my holster, my service revolver off the
coat hook by the door where I hung it when I come in. I
woulda been more prepared, but on duty or not, Connie
don't like me wearing it around the house.

JOEY Stewy got the worst of it. This one shard of window
glass hit him along the side of the head.

DENNY Time I limped out to the road, I saw the back end of
this late-model Le Mans, no plates, hauling off, the back
bumper tied on with rope and I know it was a Le Mans for

sure 'cause me and Joey, as kids we used to hang out on
the Dan Ryan overpasses and ID cars by their taillights. I
was always better at it than Joey, no contest. I got off a shot
or two. Maybe three or four. Heat of the moment, yunno,
I don't remember. I just wanted to put out a tire, shatter
the back window and the back of the motherfucker's skull
too maybe. But all I did was ticked the plastic of one of
them taillights so it glowed a glint of white out one side
of the red like this demon eyeball. Then it vanished.

JOEY   What really made Denny nuts that night was Stewy
wasn't crying. He was just sitting on the couch, all this
glass, the whole side of his head this slick of red, his
pajamas soaked with it.

DENNY   I thought: Jesus Christ, no, the glass went into his head.

JOEY   He backhanded Connie for some reason.

DENNY   She went fuckin' berserk on me! Hello!

JOEY   I called 911 but instead of waiting for an ambulance,
Denny told Connie to get Noel out into the squad car.

DENNY   I grabbed Stewy away from Joey and wrapped him up
in a blanket 'cause I figured a legitimate emergency, I use
the siren, the lights, I can get him to Masonic Hospital
faster than any fuckin' ambulance, right? That's logical,
isn't that logical?

JOEY   There was a Cubs game that night. Traffic was terrible.

DENNY   I mean, what is it with some people? I got a
legitimate emergency on the seat next to me here and
they know the law, they see the blues, hear the siren, and
still the self-absorbed motherfuckers don't pull over!
Everybody in so much a hurry to get someplace, they

think fifteen seconds sooner makes all the difference!?
Fuckin' nuts is what it is.

JOEY   Talk about nuts, it was nuts too the way Denny
wouldn't let me or Connie hold Stewy while he was at the
wheel, crazier the way he was driving, up on sidewalks,
playing chicken with pedestrians. Even me, working the
streets, I'd never seen so much blood. The blanket Denny
had wrapped around Stewy was soaked like a sponge
and Denny, driving like a madman, one-handed. Three
people were hurt in that collision with the ambulance he
caused when he charged a red light, the very ambulance
that was on its way to help us, but Denny didn't care. I
was in the back with my arms around Connie and Noel,
trying to talk them into keeping their breathing steady
so they don't hyperventilate. And no way Denny had to
slug Connie like that to settle the argument, either. She
wasn't anywhere near berserk. She sided with me. That's
what ticked him off. She wanted him to wait for the
ambulance, he wanted to drive. Denny had to do things
his way. By the time we got Stewy into emergency at
Masonic he was in shock.

DENNY   I hand Stewy over to the nurse and the way Connie's
looking at me, gashes on her arms, cut on her lip, it's like
she's going into shock on me, too, like it's all my fuckin'
fault or something. I mean their faces, Noel, too, they're
looking at me, blood draining from their faces, blue lips
and shivering, your own family, you're not God, not even
a fuckin' friend of his, you can only do what you can
fuckin' do, yunno?

JOEY Doctor came out after a few hours and told us the glass severed the artery along the side of Stewy's neck and they had no way of knowing the effects, not till he comes out of anesthesia. He was critical but stable. Some nerve damage, maybe some brain damage. The doctors weren't a hundred percent sure. Under two years old it's hard to assess. Connie, she wanted to stay at the hospital the whole night but when they wouldn't let her stay by Stewy in intensive care she went a little—

DENNY A little? She was fuckin' hysterical. And choosing this opportune moment to ride my ass, all a sudden Joey's the only one she'll listen to. He talked her into going home eventually.

(The lights change.)

JOEY It took a long time to get Noel to sleep. He kept telling Denny, "I'm scared, Daddy, don't go."

DENNY Little shit wouldn't even let me turn out the fuckin' lights.

JOEY So after Denny lost patience . . .

DENNY I fuckin' spanked him. He's my kid. You do 'em no fuckin' favors raising 'em to be tit-glomming mama's boys, believe me.

JOEY . . . I went into Noel's room, put him up on my lap, read him a few stories, talked him down, while Denny called the incident in.

DENNY And, I'm sorry, it's a blood thing. Joey'll tell you I got obsessed. Maybe I did. But a wolf, any animal'll kill to protect its young. What are you gonna tell a wolf tearing

out your jugular 'cause you're fuckin' with its kids? You're
obsessed, Mr. Big-Bad, see a shrink, little couch time, get
over it? Joey, he should be teaching Buddhism to Lutherans,
him and his slippery fuckin' slope. So I shake down a
half-dozen hookers working the North Avenue bridge once
or twice a week. They got cash to spare and plenty of ways
to make up for lost income. I turn a head, permit human
nature to progress its merry way, I keep the pimps off their
backs, they stay freelance, and everybody's happy. Serve and
protect, that's what I do. If not a plainclothes promotion,
why not a little under-the-counter compensation for going
above and beyond the call of duty on a regular basis?

JOEY Slippery slope, Den.

DENNY It's a community. I take care of them, they take care
of me. Everybody gets along. Joey and me, though, we
don't always see eye to fuckin' eye on this, but I tell the
hard-liner, soon's you find yourself a nice girl, settle down,
pop a few long balls over the fence onto Waveland Avenue
off your own bat, the world'll look entirely different, my
friend. Yunno what he tells me?

JOEY Kids or no, it's still a slippery slope, Denny.

DENNY My kid was hurt. One of my babies. It's something in
the blood way beyond logic. Spill my kid's blood, you spill
my blood. It gets my blood up, I can't help it. I filed a
report on this drive-by, the make, the model, no plates,
right taillight ticked like the eye of a demon and, sure,
Dickerson, the yobber tells me follow protocol,
Lombardo, let the dicks handle it.

JOEY We were already skating on thin ice being over at
Denny's when we should've been out on duty. Top of that,

using the squad car to get Stewy to Masonic, the accident
along the way?

DENNY Hey, it's not like it coulda been avoided or anything.
I mean, Christ, it was my kid's life on the line. I told him:
yessir, Captain Dickerson, proper channels, Captain
Dickerson, everything by the book, Captain Dickerson.
Like I'm gonna leave the safety of my family in the hands
of the fuckin' quota squad. Fuck that shit.

JOEY Denny pulled the slug from a .44 Magnum out of the
plaster behind his TV and sure, the dicks were pissed he
messed with their crime scene. But Denny told them:

DENNY This is my effing house and my effing TV and I do
what the eff I want with the effing things in it. Capiche,
gentlemen?

JOEY A .44 Magnum could've been used by any number of
characters Denny and I encounter on patrol. But the most
likely scenario, Denny tells me . . .

DENNY It's that spineless ratfuck Walter Lorenz.

JOEY The pimp Denny beats up on a semi-regular basis for
whaling on Rhonda.

(The lights change.)

DENNY Pimps, it's like a job requirement, these guys.
First, they got to be ugly as catshit and second they got
themselves convinced they're God's gift to womankind.
Okay, so most guys foot that bill. But on top it, pimps got
this smell about 'em. I call it moral rot. You can actually
smell the putrid way they think wafting off of them like
rotten flesh. I mean, they honestly think they're helping

these girls when actually they keep them enslaved, if not
with drugs, with fear, and they reek of it. I mean, if they
really wanted to help 'em, they'd do like Joey suggests
and put 'em through beauty school or secretary school,
something respectable, yunno? But pimps, this pimp
mentality, what do they do? They take potshots at my
family through my fuckin' front window.

(*The lights change.*)

JOEY   While Denny had it out with the detectives, I tried to
calm down Connie. She was a nervous wreck. I told her
try laying off the Valium, but after Denny chased out the
dicks, he told her she needed another and poured her half
a glass of scotch to chase it down. By the time I finished
reading "The Three Billy Goats Gruff" the fifth time to
Noel, the twenty-four-hour board-up guys were over
chipping out the glass and nailing huge sheets of plywood
up over what was left of Denny's front window. I heard
Denny out in the front yard in the rain shouting at the
board-up guys. He was pissed they had their company name
and phone number across the plywood in red ink and he
was bickering with them about how much he was planning
to bill them for the advertising. Connie was woozy from
the Valium, the scotch, and she walked in on me in Noel's
room, just as Noel was drifting off to sleep in my arms.

   She waved me out of the room. I tucked Noel into bed
and slipped out into the hallway. There, Connie
whispered to me that the doctor had pulled her aside
and told her that if Denny would have waited for the

ambulance, Stewy's blood loss could have been less severe
and that the possible brain and nerve damage might have
been reparable, if not preventable altogether. It was all a
lot of maybes and I told Connie so and she said she knows
but Denny does this all the time. He thinks he can do
everything himself. She told me about his leg. Denny
refused to go to the doctor for it. That's the way he was.
He wouldn't take any money from Connie's mom and
dad for the house, the down payment, the mortgage,
anything. No, Connie told me, Denny insisted on
working two, sometimes three jobs to make ends meet.

Denny never worked any two or three jobs. He barely
worked the one. Unless you count in shaking down
hookers and tavern keepers as sidelines. He'd stay out late
and tell Connie he was moonlighting. And even though
I knew Denny was out dicking around, putz that I am,
I always covered for him. He was my best friend. My
partner. Always back to back, me and Den. I'd been
covering for him for so long, I couldn't keep all the lies
straight anymore. So I told her. "Denny's not working any
two or three jobs, Con." "All that money," she asks me.
"Where's he getting it, Joey?" I didn't answer right off. "I
don't want to know, do I?" she says. I say: "He's taking care
of his family." Connie's laugh was full of disgust. "This
fat lip he gave me is taking care of his family? A bullet
through our front window is taking care of his family?
Stewy—?"

Connie kind of broke down and slumped into my
arms. As I held her in the hallway that night to comfort
her, it dawned on me why all the women I'd dated over

the years had faded out of my life with a shrug. Holding
Connie, the light, it gave me a strength I never had alone.
She had no way of knowing it, but it was her gave me the
strength to be comforting. She's always telling me I'm so
good to Denny, so good to her, so good to the kids, Heinz
even. But it's Connie, really. She has that kind of effect on
me. It all comes from her. Always has.

   With Stewy's life in the balance, everything kind
of opened up between us that night. I think Connie
suspected the worst before I ratted Denny out. She just
put up with Denny's bullshit for the sake of the kids. Plus
she loved him, too. I stood up at their wedding, no doubt
about that. Connie could forgive Denny anything. For
clocking her like he did, cutting her lip with that stupid
faux Super Bowl pinky ring of his. She loved him that
much. I did too, I guess. Kids, he'd beat the crap out of
me daily. Summers, three times a day, more if we were
really bored. I'd never cry or complain about it because if
I did I was afraid Denny would stop being my best friend.
The thought of that hurt worse than anything.

   The board-up guys gone, Denny limped up the stairs.
It wasn't me holding Connie that got him suspicious as
much as the fact that me and Connie both, we pulled
away from each other the same second. We stood there off
balance, this cloud of shame hanging between us because
we both ratted Denny out and without exactly meaning
to do so, allied against him. You know how you know
someone so well, you can read them in an instant? Denny
read the guilt on us as easy as we could read the suspicion
in him.

I stayed on the couch that night. I'd done it a lot, lately. Even though I suspected he'd like to toss me out on my ear, Denny thought it was a good idea I play watchdog. Heinz was hiding under the bed in Noel's room and wouldn't come out. So I stood guard in case Walter Lorenz came back with something more potent than a .44 Magnum.

(*Fade.*)

4

Lights rise on JOEY *and* DENNY.

JOEY Next day out on patrol was one of those days you dread.
Denny wasn't talking. Usually he breezes on and on, this
and that, never a lull. But that day he was so quiet it made
me sweat the seat. I thought, sure, he's yanked about
Stewy, the bullet through the window, the TV. I'd be,
too. But it was like Connie herself was sitting in the front
seat between us. (*Pause.* JOEY *adjusts himself in his seat.*)
Tail end of our shift, around one a.m., a call came in,
routine disorderly in an alley behind an apartment
complex near Broadway and Sheridan, the part of town
Denny called Deviant Corners. Usually, I look to Denny
for the nod before I take the call because, you know, on
any given patrol he's got his set routine, this set number
of shakedown homies to stop and see. But that night I did
like I'm supposed to do. I responded, said we'd check it
out. Without a word, Denny turned around the squad car
and floored it up Halsted to Broadway.

DENNY So Joey and me, we pull up this alley off Deviant
Corners. Right away in the headlights is this kid, this kid,
this Vietnamese kid, stoned out of his fuckin' mind. Not a
stitch of clothes. He's fumbling through the garbage cans,
trying first to climb 'em and then to stack 'em up and

make like this stairway to heaven over a tall, wood fence. He climbs up, the rotten planks of the fence give, he falls, dipshit does it again.

JOEY Never a dull moment this neck of the woods.

DENNY They import spices from all corners of the world at Deviant Corners. Deviations psychiatrists ain't even identified yet. Me and Joey, we keep the headlights on the kid, train the side spot on him, half the neighborhood grandstanding out their windows both sides and up above the alley watching this naked kid stumbling around doing this pony show with the alley rats. We draw our service revolvers 'cause any cop, you see somebody out of control this way, distressed or not, it's usually PCP . . .

JOEY X . . .

DENNY Crack . . .

JOEY H . . .

DENNY Some whacked-out cocktail, you never fuckin' know.

JOEY So you play it safe.

DENNY We go to him slow, cautious.

JOEY He turns, sees us.

DENNY Me and Joey, we can see the kid's in tears, verge of hysteria just about. And the third world ding-dong comes running at us like that 'Nam photo. Yunno, that girl running naked from the napalm blitzkrieg.

JOEY Kim.

DENNY Exactly like Kim. Only toting a little more baggage up front.

JOEY Tears running down his face, yammering a mile a minute in Vietnamese about something woeful.

DENNY Who the fuck knows? You think napalm's bad? You
ain't seen half the shit in this city I seen. I seen kids lit on
fire by their own parents.

JOEY He slobbers up to us, ignoring any order we toss him.

DENNY Fascist bullshit, yunno: down on the ground,
facedown. Despite the bead I got on him, the whacked-out
skibby ducks under my gun arm and gloms onto me. Locks
his arms around me. The rice puppy's fuckin' hugging me
and, 'course, I don't shoot. I mean, I can see he's unarmed
and the kid, Christ, he's singing the Vietnamese blues to
me, putting the squeeze on me so hard it actually brought
the steak burrito I had for dinner back up the pipeline. And
I look over to Joey for a little assistance here, but Joey don't
speak dinky-doo any more than I do. So Joey tells me . . .

JOEY Try and calm the kid down while I go to the car for a
blanket.

DENNY And, I dunno, what do you do to calm this kid down,
sing him a Vietnamese lullaby? He's like thirteen or
fourteen and he's naked. I mean, I can't hug him back. So
I'm standing there like a jerk, both arms in the air, this
naked kid glomming onto me in the rain, all these people
watching from the windowsill bleachers overhead, till
Joey, like eight hours later, finally comes back with the
fuckin' blanket out the fuckin' trunk and wraps the kid in
it. Joey practically had to peel the kid off of me. Christ, it
was like he was superglued to my midsection, like he was
like fuckin' one with me or something.

JOEY We pried him loose eventually. Trying to talk him
down and getting nowhere, this beefy blond guy, he

looked like a surfer, he comes up to us from outta one
of the basement apartments off of the alley carrying a
yellow umbrella and says he'll take care of Li-Yao.

DENNY He tells us the kid's name is Li-Yao. He's from
Vietnam, sure enough, and he's his nephew or cousin or
both. I forgot what he said exactly. But I do remember he
said the kid had some kinda war trauma and sleeping,
bathing, drop of a hat, the surfer guy told us, Li-Yao flips
out and thinks he's being dinky-gy-ponged all over again.

JOEY Which made sense at the time.

DENNY You can't run the kid in for being traumatized.
Ninety-nine percent of this fuckin' city is traumatized.

JOEY So Denny tells me . . .

DENNY Release him to his uncle's custody and let's amscray,
uh? Joey didn't wanna do it at first.

JOEY Li-Yao seemed scared to death of his uncle.

DENNY But, hell, we couldn't understand a word he was
saying. How the fuck were we supposed to know?

JOEY Denny saw a late-model Le Mans pull into the gas
station off the alley and wanted to check it out. I told him
I thought maybe we should bring the kid and his uncle in,
maybe hunt down an interpreter, check out what the kid's
saying. Denny told me . . .

DENNY Fine, J. Play Mother Teresa. Save the world. I got
official police business to conduct.

JOEY . . . and took off for the squad car. The kid, Li-Yao, he
went limp in my arms. I had to actually catch him, hold
him up. The guy, the one who said he was the uncle, he
told me this is what happens when Li-Yao's posttraumatic

stress disorder medication finally kicks in. So I'm standing there with this passed-out naked kid in my arms, Denny's marching off to play *Death Wish* on whoever took a potshot through his window, I don't know what to do. So I handed Li-Yao over to his uncle. The guy seemed nice enough. I looked him square in the eye to get a read. He seemed decent. He really did.

Time I got over to the gas station, Denny was already confronting the man driving the Le Mans, a Puerto Rican gentleman, mid-twenties maybe. He was coming out of the convenience mart of the Citgo, bag of chips, can of pop, and Denny, not even a greeting, he steps in front smashing the guy's chips between them. Not the most cordial way to begin a friendly little conversation, but that's Denny. The Puerto Rican gentleman winds up to take a poke, but reeled it back in when he saw Denny's badge and uniform.

Denny asks the guy, he calls him "Rico" and, you know, I try to correct Denny about doing people this way, but this particular night, he was nuts, I swear. He accuses me not only of being against free speech, but of trying to leach the testosterone out of the law. He asks the guy, he says, one: "Are you a friend of Walter Lorenz?" and two: "Had any tail work done recently, Rico?" And the guy, Rico, they do this sometimes, all of a sudden he can't speak English in his own country. He says to Denny: "Cómo, pendejo?" Which means something, I think, like: "What, pubic hair?" And Denny, both of us have been out on the streets long enough to pick up a little cha-cha, he's got a vague idea it's not so nice so he shoves the guy up against the Le Mans.

Rico's pop goes sailing, chips scatter, and Denny knifes the guy with a roundhouse sidewinder to the left kidney. Lower back, you know, real danger spot. Soon as I saw that I knew there's more than official police business going down here. So I step in and grab Denny by the wrist just as he's pawing his belt for his joystick to clomp the guy, you know, just to remind him to follow protocol because you get out of hand these days, these things can come back to haunt you, and we're already skating on thin ice as it is. Denny flicks me off, shoves *me* up against the Le Mans and plants his joystick with both hands across my throat, pinning me to the car. "Was it *your* family got shot at? Was it *your* wife? Was it *your* kids?" He says: "No, Joey! It's *my* family! *My* kids! *My* wife! *Mine!*" He made his point and eventually backed off. Good thing, too, because I was just about to lift a knee and take Denny down the hard way. He was my best friend and all, I love the guy, but I'm not about to stand around and let him treat me like this, accusing me of things he's got no right accusing me.

I told Rico to get in his car and go. He hauls off into traffic shouting something back at Denny and me with the word "loco" in it. I didn't catch the rest.

DENNY It wasn't "vios con dios," believe me.

JOEY Denny just glared at me, not a twitch. I told him: "Go sit in the car, Den. Relax. I'll get us some coffees." I've never seen him so still. But he did what I told him. I went into the mart, bought us coffees, cream, Sweet'N Low, and when I walk out, I'm almost up to the squad car, Denny hauls off and leaves me there. Here I am, on duty, my best friend, my partner leaves me holding two hot coffees at this Deviant Corners gas station in the pouring rain.

(*Fade.*)

5

Lights rise on DENNY.

DENNY A man has every right to do anything it takes to
protect his family, and what are cops for if not to get out
and remind people they can't take the law into their own
hands? Detectives, Jesus, if we left it up to the dicks
nothing'd get done 'cause they don't know the streets, they
don't know people. Half their cases they follow paper
trails. They're garbagemen, glorified desk clerks, more
concerned with dreaming up new ways to clock OT than
preserving law and order. Top of that, what am I supposed
to do? Hang out at Masonic sitting on my thumbs and
drinking bad machine coffee like that'll help bring my kid
Stewy back from brain damage?

So this Puerto Rican stiff at the Citgo, I walked up
to him very polite, I asked him: "Excuse me, sir, I'd like
to ask you a few questions about your whereabouts last
evening." And like that, he drops his groceries, lunges for
his car, and drives off. My partner, Joey, he's off dealing
with this alleyway incident across the street. So, no time to
call him, I go after this Puerto Rican gentleman. I mean,
hey, running like hell from a cop is usually a pretty
persuasive indicator something ugly's amuck. Following
this guy's taillights, we hit the Outer Drive. Guy was this
close. I'm indicating every which way I can to pull the

hell over, and what does he do? Pouring rain, he tries to jump the concrete embankment doing 80, flips his car over two or three times and lands it upside down thirty feet below the S-curve overpass. Sure, I woulda called in for backup, followed protocol to the letter, cut the guy off, but Joey, he's out on another call and I only got two hands driving, I mean, I didn't wanna 'cause any more accidents or anything. I was in trouble enough.

The guy died in the wreck. I dunno how the side of my squad car got scraped up but it definitely was not from knocking the Puerto Rican gentleman off the road in the middle of a high-speed chase down Lake Shore Drive. The dicks can speculate all they like. These things are simply not done. It was the guy's own fault. I blamed it on the rain. Sole survivor of the altercation: Last Man Standing. Dicks had to file my story, no matter how many fuckin' holes they tried to poke through it, the token prick assholes.

Afterwards, I swing back by the Citgo and Joey, he's nowhere to be found. So I ring home to ask Connie has she heard from the deadbeat 'cause I figured maybe he'd dingaling her and ask her has she maybe heard from me.

(*Lights rise on* JOEY.)

DENNY Sonuvabitch answers. This doesn't surprise me, but it surprised me. I mean, Joey, nobody knows this, I virtually brought the guy back from the dead he drank so bad. You know a guy's got it bad for the bottle, 'cause when he gets it alone, nothing else matters. You know how many times

I covered for that guy, signed in for him, covered his beat?
I can't even count. That fucked-up mick was in a free-fall
tailspin till I concocted the plan for his salvation. He
shaped up, knocked off the sauce completely. It was a
good change to see. A good change to count myself part
of. But the way things got, it was like he was always fuckin'
there, yunno, even when you didn't want him to be.
And, sure, he's like my brother, I love the guy, but the
sonuvabitch can be the biggest pain in the ass sometimes.

So I hung up. I knew where the ratfuck was. Fine. On
my way home, I thought I'd do some networking, ask a few
questions, scare up a few leads. I mean, time the dicks crack
this one, we'll all be dead. So I ran into Rhonda, talked to
her in a bar for an hour or two, bought her a drink, pumped
her for a little information, and she says to me, she says:
"Secretary school? Denny, I can't do secretary school. I got
a fuckin' kid to take care of." I told her: "Lemme do the
taking care of. I'm good for day care. I'll front your tuition,
too." She was grateful but skeptical. She appreciated my
concern. And I don't know what happened to me, maybe
all this stress lately. I only had like three or four beers and it
hit me hard giving her a lift home. So I pulled over into
Waveland Park and just kinna knocked off.

JOEY Denny went off the deep end that night. Me and a
couple of other cops, Varallo and Meese, found him
parked out on the flooded ninth hole of the Waveland
Golf Course. He said he only had two or three beers. But
it takes more than that to tank Denny. A lot more. I found
a couple spent vials of morphine and a syringe in a nearby
sand trap. When we carried him into his house, into the

light, I could tell he'd been with Rhonda again. I could see it in Connie's face she knew, too. Denny's pants were on inside out. Connie told us to put him on the foldout on the back porch. In case he chucked cheese, it's the only place in the house besides the kitchen not shagged. Connie and me sat up most the night drinking coffee in the kitchen. I called every hour to Masonic to check on Stewy. The same, they told me, the same, like the weather report, always the same.

Waiting. Waiting, waiting, waiting. That's what that summer was about. An excruciating exercise in patience. Waiting for Stewy to take a turn for the better. Waiting for things to blow sky-high between Denny and me. Waiting for an end to the rain. A lighter air. A brighter sky. Then they caught the psycho guy, this cannibal worse than anything anybody'd ever seen in the movies, and it turned out the Vietnamese boy Li-Yao was one of his victims.

DENNY No sooner do the papers, the news flash the guy's picture, than the boards are lit up with a million or more calls, witnesses the night these two dipshit beat cops turned this crying Vietnamese kid over to the cannibal killer. I mean, parts of this kid's body have still not been found. I told Dickerson, I said: "Just 'cause you and your dicks can't find his heart and liver, don't necessarily mean they been eaten." I'd like to meet the reporter came up with the cannibal tag. It's always assuming the worse with some people. I'd have a serious talk with that yobber about logic, yunno?

JOEY Denny thought the dicks had it out for us. There were countless times he'd interfered with their work. Not in a bad way. Out on patrol, Denny'd turn a clue or two that would actually help them out, help them solve some cases. Then they'd take him to task for it. Not 'cause Denny tried to take the credit. He never did. Mostly 'cause the dicks resented being shown up by a stupid beat cop. When they caught this cannibal killer, instead of piecing together a case, they spent most of the early part of their investigation tying Denny and me to Li-Yao. Going to that length to ID a couple of scapegoats sure made it seem like Dickerson and his rank-and-file dick squad were out to nail us.

DENNY I mean, I got kids to raise in this world and these blousy fucks are gonna hold me responsible for this madman? Where the hell is the logic in that? Without a common logic, it's every man for himself and fuck your neighbor as you would expect your neighbor to fuck unto you. Is this a civilization or what?

JOEY At first, Dickerson suspended us both with pay. Week later, after the press got ahold of it, we were suspended without pay. Which whacked our chances for appeal. Our F.O.P. advocates, the guys who helped me and Denny remove the racial-slur reprimands from our files, all hands-off suddenly like something or somebody got to 'em. Dickerson offered us a deal. If we admitted breaching protocol by not running Li-Yao in, he promised us reinstatement in a month. Denny didn't want to admit any wrongdoing.

DENNY I mean, some asshole takes a potshot through my front window, just about kills my kid, and they want me to turn in my badge, turn in my service revolver, the only

protection I got? It's the logic, see, the logic is wanting.
A beat cop job description, they don't demand fuckin'
omniscience. Like at how many paces can you identify a
serial killer who eats his victims' hearts. I mean, how the
hell were we supposed to know?

JOEY But I talked him into it. For his kids' sake, for Connie's.
We signed this statement, and not two days later, the
cannibal killer decides to issue a complete, horrifying
confession. Papers run the whole thing.

DENNY Fuckin' Dickerson reneged on the deal.

JOEY Too much pressure from the press. They let me and
Denny fry.

DENNY The surfer guy said he was the kid's uncle. We
believed he was his uncle. Christ, the kid was glomming
on me. I don't know Asian! Kids of my own, don't you
think this eats me up? I still see his face, all the time his
face, and I walk around, awake, asleep, I still feel his arms
around me like I was his last saving grace and I fuckin'
failed him. Ain't that punishment enough?

JOEY Denny took it hard. Especially with things so touch-and-
go with Stewy, Denny definitely did not need this. He
collapsed inside. His drinking got worse than ever. I called
him on the track marks up and down his arm, he told me
mosquito bites.

DENNY I see that look in Noel's face. In Connie's face. In
Stewy's face when I go to visit him, looking up at me
through all them spaghetti tubes and wires. And all I'm
fuckin' trying to do, like any other man, is take care of my
family. Why take away my means to do that? Why? Even
my name, my face, all over the news, the papers, who the

fuck is gonna hire me to do shit in this town now? For
precisely what purpose am I being crucified over here?!

JOEY I hated seeing Denny like that so I got on the horn to
any attorney who'd talk to me. I asked about mine and
Denny's chances of fighting this suspension thing in
court.

DENNY Sure, the shitheel Joey digs up, he tells me just go
along with what Dickerson says or I'll make things worse,
we'll sue for back pay, we'll sue for damages. Be patient.
Wait. But I ask the shyster motherfucker what about now!?
I gotta make a safe, secure home for my family! I got no
ambition bigger than that! My kids, my family, my wife!
That's who I am! That's all I'll let anybody hold me
responsible for! The shyster tells me I'm right. What's
been done to me and Joey is not fair, we got a good case,
we'll win, but winning takes time. Time, I tell him, right:
as if this hourly shyster in suspenders and a comb-over
works *pro boner.*

JOEY The attorney me and Denny finally went to see wanted
to depose us separately, take down our stories, standard
homicide procedure, see how the facts match up. They
didn't, apparently. When me and Denny went to see this
guy together, he told us no matter what our individual
stories, the facts of the case were two cops took the call
on this Vietnamese kid and one of you turned him over
to his killer. There's unquestionable fault here, he told
us, dereliction of duty, poor judgment. Everything the
internal-affairs investigation labeled it, our attorney felt,
was not unwarranted. So I ask him: "What are you saying?
We don't have a case?"

DENNY And he says . . .

JOEY "One of you has a case."

DENNY "But one of you has to take the fall."

JOEY "I strongly recommend you retain separate attorneys."

DENNY Separate attorneys, the shit-eating shyster tells us.
Me and Joey, we're like brothers, he wants to pit us one
against the other just to get one of us his job back! 'Cause
the world is such an irredeemable shit hole, one of our
two asses has to be nailed out to dry? Where's the logic in
this? 'Cause the world is bubbling over with bloodshed,
'cause madmen fuck kids and eat their livers, bury their
victims by the droves under their suburban houses, light
them on fire, take potshots at two-year-olds through their
front windows, one of us two should be fed to the wolves?
Sacrificed to what? For what? Is this some fuckin' pagan
ritual here or the United States of America? I'm missing
the logic here entirely.

(*Fade.*)

6

Lights rise on JOEY *and* DENNY.

JOEY I told Denny I'd take the fall. We could go with any
story he wanted. His call, whatever. After all, Stewy's
hospital bills were huge and Connie hadn't planned on
going back to selling real estate till he started preschool.
Sure, she could find something now, but Denny, he
needed to be the provider. I don't mean that as a put-
down. One thing we agreed on: Denny *was* his family. He
needed them to need him. And what the hell was I? This
single, interloping putz in love with his best friend's wife.
Everything, it shattered, soon's I put that name on it. I
could call what I felt for Connie other things, sure. But
why waltz around it? I was as much a threat to the safety
and security of Denny's home as any faceless serial killer
strolling the streets. I was more of a threat because I was
on the inside.

Me out the picture, it would be a timely turnaround
for Denny. We weren't looking at hard time or anything.
I'd simply take the rap and leave town. Move to Seattle or
someplace with mountains. I've always had a thing for
mountains even though I've never seen any up close and
personal. But then I thought: Seattle, Jesus, doesn't it rain
like every other effing day there? And the last thing I
needed was more rain because that summer, that's all

there was. Just rain and more rain. Endless rain like
something holding back had finally opened up. There was
even a TV evangelist kept saying this serial killer, all this
rain, it was the beginning of the end, the Deluge.

DENNY So Joey comes to me like Christ toting his own cross
to shoulder the whole rap. No way, I told him. I'd kill him
first. Even had to beat the living shit out of him like the
old days just to prove my point.

JOEY Denny and me had a little scuffle. I was getting the
worst of it, as usual, so I pounded Denny on his sore leg. I
never heard him scream like that before. He went down
like a wet rag. We were outside his house and had slapped
each other around quite a bit, grass burns, bruises, and
mud from head to foot, our clothes ripped to shreds. I saw
the hole in his thigh through his torn pants. Whatever he
did to his leg was infected. Worse. His thigh was green
and black from the knee to his hip. I tried to get him to
the doctor. But he took off in his car.

The hospital people called right after that and said
Stewy had a complication, some clotting they needed
to relieve and they needed Denny and Connie down at
Masonic immediately to discuss the procedure, the risks,
and sign a consent. Denny gone, Connie asked me to go
with her. That was the first night I kissed her.

It was like all this stress pushed us together. I don't
know how else to say it. The worst thing I could have
done I did at the worst possible time and I just let it
happen and blamed it on the rain. Everything was so
oppressive and gray and Connie was the only daylight I'd
seen in weeks, I swear. I called everywhere looking for

Denny. No luck. There was nothing more we could
do at Masonic. One signature was enough to okay the
procedure on Stewy, and after they did it, it was limbo
again, waiting and more waiting till the anesthesia wore
off. So this nurse came out and told us, she said: "We
won't know anything till morning. You may as well go
home and rest, Mr. and Mrs. Lombardo." Neither Connie
or I corrected her. We just walked out of the hospital
hand-in-hand, Noel asleep on my shoulder.

After we put Noel to bed, we kissed outside his closed
door, the same place we first held each other. I didn't start
it, she didn't start it. We both just fell into it and couldn't
let go. She took me by the hand to the bedroom, Denny's
bedroom, Denny's bed, and it wasn't just lust. We both
needed to be inside something other than our own skins
that night. Curled around each other listening to the rain
drumming on the roof, neither one of us could sleep.
There was a bright flash of lightning and I shot up in bed.
I swore I saw Denny standing in the bedroom doorway.

I got dressed and looked around. But I didn't see
anything. Connie thought I was crazy. Den was limping
so bad lately, we would have heard him come in. She told
me come back to bed. But I couldn't. I went to look for
him. I had an idea where he might be.

When I got to the Dan Ryan overpass down by the old
neighborhood where we grew up, sure enough there was
Denny. He was sitting in a puddle where the concrete
sloped watching the northbound traffic. Soaked to the
skin, he was wearing his range revolver. Even when I sat

down next to him, he wouldn't look at me. He reached
into his lap and tossed me a thick wad of money. A lot of
money. I don't know how much. I didn't count it, but it
was a thick stack of hundreds. He says to me . . .

DENNY Go buy an attorney.

JOEY Where'd you get this?

DENNY I got it.

JOEY The coke and the heroin in the trunk, I thought.
Them bangers we busted. Denny never brought it
in, never logged it as evidence. He was still doing the
morphine. He had a bottle next to him, too, a fifth of JD,
half empty.

DENNY Half full. (DENNY *laughs*.) Taillights on some of these
late models glare at you like the eyes of demons, Joey.
Think you'd know the eyes of a demon if you saw one?

JOEY We didn't know, Denny. First thing we've got to do to
face this thing is let ourselves off the hook. We didn't
know.

DENNY But we should know, Joey. We should know the eyes
of a demon when we see one.

JOEY We can't know. How can we know?

DENNY It's our job. Otherwise we end up with demons for
friends.

(*Pause.*)

JOEY Were you home tonight, Den?

DENNY Home? I ain't been home in hours, J. Hours and
hours. Days. Weeks. Months. Years.

JOEY You saw us together, didn't you?

DENNY Saw who together?

(JOEY *grabs* DENNY *by the shirt, pulls him close.*)

JOEY You were there in the doorway, Denny! Don't fuck
around! I saw you!

DENNY My ears, please. I'm sensitive.

(JOEY *releases* DENNY. DENNY *stares off at the passing traffic
hissing hollowly on the wet pavement below.*)

JOEY We sat there in that rain for, I don't know, an hour,
longer, not a word, just Denny mumbling the makes and
models of passing cars under his breath. When he spotted
the Le Mans from the overpass, he hobbled off to his car
and I followed him. Denny had his Plymouth ditched on
the northbound embankment. I jumped in the passenger
door just as he gunned the motor.

DENNY They want heroes, Joey. Be a hero. That's the way to
get reinstated. Superhuman, that's what they want us to
be. Able to tell good from evil in a blink. That's what they
want, that's what they get.

JOEY He's going on like this, weaving through traffic, topping
ninety in pursuit of this late-model Le Mans with taillights
he swears glare at him like the eyes of a demon. I'm trying
to slow him down but how can you? Denny overtook the
Le Mans and motioned it over. There was a kid at the
wheel, gangbanger brat in a Raiders cap. He could hardly
see over the wheel. Denny knew him from somewhere.

DENNY It was Willy.

JOEY On suspension, we had no badges, no squad car, no
siren to show we're cops. All Denny could think to do to
make his point more emphatic was to wave Willy over
with his range revolver.

DENNY Willy saw the gun and veered off west.

JOEY Denny stuck with him for another mile or more until
he forced him off the road and Willy flipped the Le Mans
in a Forest Preserve cul-de-sac.

DENNY Then bolted out the wreck and into the woods.

JOEY He was wearing one of those gangbanger warm-up
jackets and had something tucked inside it, in the front.

DENNY A .44.

JOEY Denny waved me to stay behind him when we chased
Willy into the Forest Preserve.

DENNY Joey was unarmed.

JOEY He didn't want me hurt.

DENNY Willy tripped and turfed nose-first in a clearing.

JOEY He was messing with whatever he had in his coat when
Denny caught up with him and ordered him hands out of
the pockets and lay facedown on the ground.

DENNY Willy was scared shitless.

JOEY He was doing what Denny said but all of a sudden he
unzipped part of his coat and reached in and, I'm sorry,
you just can't do that around a cop.

DENNY Not a fast, jerky motion like that.

JOEY It triggers a cop.

DENNY It's training, not choice.

JOEY There's no time to think. Life or death, sometimes you
just have to react.

DENNY I didn't mean to kill him. Logical conclusion, it's a
piece in his coat, right? A .44, right? I link the car to the
shooting, Willy to Walter, ballistics on the gun'll provide the
last missing piece, case closed. But Joey, he goes to Willy, he
opens his coat and there's this fuckin' puppy inside it.

JOEY Who woulda thought he's running from the law with a
fuckin' puppy?

DENNY Joey takes the puppy and I shove him aside searching
Willy for a piece.

JOEY Willy was clean. Denny got real panicky and limped
back to the overturned Le Mans. He practically stripped
it. After he popped open the trunk with a tire iron, Denny
squirmed in and found what he wanted.

DENNY (*Muttering to himself.*) .44 Magnum . . .
.44 Magnum . . . .44 Magnum . . .

JOEY There were other guns stashed in the trunk, too. But
the .44 was what Denny wanted most. He tucked it down
Willy's pants.

DENNY And sure enough, tucked down Willy's pants is a
fuckin' .44.

JOEY Denny was a madman that night, like a man in flames.
He even wagged his range revolver at me and told me . . .

DENNY Beat it. It's my kid was hurt. This is my fuckin' collar.

JOEY I walked out of the Forest Peserve with the puppy and
flagged a cab.

I went straight to Connie with the whole story.
"Enough is enough," she said and got right on the phone
to Dickerson. I just sat there at the kitchen table, Denny's
kitchen table, Noel and Heinz playing with the puppy
on the floor in the living room, Denny's family room, the

front window still boarded up. And sitting there, I just
listened to her tell Dickerson everything. I betrayed
my friend. Again. And I felt ashamed because I was so
relieved I wouldn't have to go to Seattle and confront all
those mountains and all that rain. With Denny out the
picture, I could move right in. I'd invested whole parts
of myself in Noel, in Stewy, in Connie. They gave me a
strength I never had, made something of me that never
was. I belonged to them. Sitting there that night, I started
thinking that they belonged to me. That I had more of a
right to this family than Denny ever did.

DENNY Ballistics matched that .44 to the same gun that fired
through my front window. Registration in the glove
compartment provided a paper trail for the brilliant
dickheads to follow. Car was registered to Willy's brother,
Walter. So I land this drive-by delinquent, bring in a
cache of stolen guns, semiautomatic weapons, AK-47s and
shit, and what does Dickerson slap me with? The token
shitfuck tells me I'm under arrest. "For what?" I ask
him. "For Chrissake, Dickerson, I'm doing my job!" He
reminds me I'm on suspension so I remind that prick:
"My fuckin' kid's life is hanging by a thread and you arrest
me? I'm out busting my ass, risking my life making this
city a safer more secure place to live and you arrest me?!"
The man's logic was totally fucked. He's got kids of his
own, I'm out there being a fuckin' hero and he puts the
fuckin' bite on me? Walking out, I told him fuck him, his
fuckin' quota system, and his family, and yunno what he
says to me? He says: "We know where to find you, Den."
Sonuvabitch.

So, just to lay low, I go to Rhonda's. She's stabbed to
death in her bed. Her baby's taped up inside a plastic
garbage bag in the little bed I brought her. Knew it the
second I saw it, this is Walter Lorenz's handiwork. He did it
to get back at me for muscling in on what's his, for Willy.

When I finally tracked down the pimpshit, I chased
him best I could. My leg couldn't take much weight. I
followed him down an alley and out into the street. I ran
into a couple of cops there, Varallo and Meese. Friends of
mine, I known 'em for years. Walter's pissing his pants,
asking Varallo and Meese to protect him. I tell 'em what
Walter did to Rhonda and her kid, they don't wanna hear
it, they think I'm too ripped up, they got orders to bring
me in. So the dumb shits start reciting me my Mirandas,
Walter standing there shouting: "You popped my brother,
greaseball! You're gonna fry, motherfucker!"

It was just reflex, that's all it was. I grabbed the gun out
of Varallo's holster and pumped three chambers' worth
point-blank into Walter Lorenz before any of us could
blink. We all just stood around for a dead second or two,
stunned. I turned the gun on Varallo and Meese and
limped back down the alley to my car. Protocol, they
shoulda shot me. At least wounded me. But neither
Varallo or Meese would shoot. I was not only a friend of
theirs. I was a cop. Suspended, but I was still a cop. A cop
simply does not shoot another cop.

JOEY When Connie heard Denny pull in, she told me I
better go. Connie was worried how Denny'd take it when
she told him she called Dickerson. I told her that was
exactly the reason I better stay.

Denny walked in all smiles. He wrapped Connie up in a hug and told her she can sleep nights again because he caught the gunman who shot out their window and did what he did to Stewy. Connie just took it cold and Denny was left hanging like he was humping a post. He let her go and glared at me, something new in his eyes, a wicked flicker. Connie told him I told her about the .44. He already knew. He knew Dickerson knew. He knew the approaching siren was a car sent for him. He knew about Connie and me. He knew everything.

I could see it work on his face and the final proof drove home when he ordered me out of his house. I stood my ground.

DENNY This is *my* house, *my* wife, *my* family! You got no fuckin' right to interfere. No fuckin' right to even be here!

JOEY Noel ran to Connie and hung on to her leg. Both of them standing behind me, the battle lines drawn.

DENNY Get out.

JOEY Denny could always beat the hell out of me. I told you that. Usually, I could get a lick or two of my own in, which was always a mistake with Denny because when he fought, he was like an animal. Show any resistance, he guns at you with double the fury. As a kid, I used to just let him pound on me till he knew he had the upper hand. He'd eventually quit. But it wasn't only Connie and Noel cowering behind me in the kitchen that stopped him dead in his tracks that night. It was something in me. I finally had something worth fighting for and I wasn't about to roll over. So he lifted Varallo's service revolver to my head and cocked it.

DENNY Get out.

JOEY Shoot me if you like, Den. Just let Connie and Noel out of this.

DENNY Okay.

JOEY He pulled the trigger. It just clicked.

(DENNY *laughs*.)

JOEY Where you going with this, Denny?

(DENNY *waves* JOEY *closer.* JOEY *steps toward him. In pain,* DENNY *grabs on to* JOEY *and falls, pulling them both to their knees. They are forehead to forehead on the ground.*)

DENNY I can't protect 'em from it anymore, Joey.

JOEY I know, Denny, I know.

DENNY It's everywhere, Joey, yunno? Rhonda's dead.

JOEY I know, Den, I know.

DENNY I found her, J. Stabbed to death in her bed.

JOEY I know.

DENNY Her baby, Joey, her baby's dead, too. Tied up in a fuckin' garbage bag. I did it.

JOEY You didn't do it.

DENNY I did it.

JOEY It was Walter, Den.

DENNY It was me, Joey.

JOEY No.

DENNY I was with her.

JOEY I coulda stopped this.

DENNY No.

JOEY I shoulda.

DENNY No, I popped his kid brother. I pissed him off. I coulda capped him long before any of this went down, before Stewy got hurt, but I didn't. It's all my doing.

JOEY You can't take responsibility for it all, Denny.

DENNY I gotta.

JOEY Don't you fuckin' do this!

DENNY Family man, you gotta.

JOEY No, Den.

DENNY I brought it home with me. I can't wash it off.

JOEY Don't, Denny.

DENNY It's infected everything. It's in me, Joey.

JOEY No.

DENNY It *is* me. (*Pause.*) Take care of 'em for me, Joey.

JOEY We take care of each other, Den.

DENNY They're all I got. All I ever had.

JOEY Back-to-back. Haven't we always?

(DENNY *shoves* JOEY *away roughly.* JOEY *stands.*)

DENNY Take 'em.

JOEY I picked up Noel, led Connie out. I looked back at Denny in the dark. He was reloading Varallo's service revolver. That was me three months ago. That was me not knowing which way to point that thing. That was me blasted senseless with no light, no family, no nothing.

DENNY Hey, Joey, ten to one Dickerson reinstates you and you make detective for bringing down the bad guy single-handed.

JOEY C'mon, Denny, you coming?

DENNY Back-to-back, J. Starsky and Hutch. Like the old days.

JOEY Two steps after the screen door clacked behind Connie, me, and Noel, I heard the shot from inside.

(Please resist the impulse to fade on DENNY *here. He should remain fully lit and alive to the end. He listens to* JOEY's *story attentively to the end.)*

JOEY The Department didn't honor Denny's pension. There was no life insurance, either, because it was a suicide. When I took Connie to make arrangements for Denny's funeral, we decided to have him cremated. I don't think he would have liked the idea of lying to rot in some cold plot of dirt for all eternity any more than I do. Cremation at least saved us the cost of having his face reconstructed. He popped the gun just under his chin.

No way in hell I wanted to say what I said at my reinstatement hearing. But Connie told me: "He's dead, Joey. He's dead. Denny is dead. Let him do something good for us. He would have wanted it that way."

Bible school, I remember, Father Joel, he'd keep us waiting. Busy training altar boys or some shit. And while we were waiting, down the ravine by the train tracks behind the church, Denny'd make up these games. To pass the time. For nothing, for fun. Denny invented rock tag. He called it Last Man Standing. Plenty of rocks handy for ammo down around the track bed. The object of the game, of course, was to be the last man standing.

It was Denny ended up taking the fall for everything. Like he predicted, I came out smelling like a rose, made detective next round of promotions. I didn't think it'd look good but Connie told me she didn't give a damn what looked good or not, she needed me so I moved in. I can't say I wasn't happy to clear out of my one room, lay claim to some home cooking on a regular basis. Stewy was home from Masonic about a month after Denny died. He'll be okay, they said, with special ed, some rehab, time to heal.

The rain finally let up. Everything looked and smelled cleansed. Finally got around to replace the family-room window, too.

It's strange the things you've got to lose to gain this much. I mean, Denny was a part of me, gone forever. Out walking Heinz and Heinz Junior at night, I go by the house from the street and see them lit up and framed in the big new family-room window: Connie and the kids. My family. Such a simple picture. I know what Denny felt seeing it. I'd do anything for them.

Anything.

(JOEY *and* DENNY *exchange a look. Blackout.*)

9 780865 479364